Real-World Math

Grades 1–2

Strengthen the Math Skills
Needed in Everyday Life

Fresh-Squeezed Lemonade
Today 12:00-2:00

Large (20 oz.) - 25¢
Medium (10 oz.) - 15¢
Small (5 oz.) - 10¢

by Susan Carroll

Carson-Dellosa Publishing Company, Inc.

Greensboro, North Carolina

Credits

Editor
Susan Morris

Layout Design
Jon Nawrocik

Artists
Van Harris
Jon Nawrocik

Cover Design
Annette Hollister-Papp

Cover and Inside Photos
Photo www.comstock.com
© 1993 Digital Wisdom, Inc.
© 2001 Brand X Pictures
© 1999 EyeWire, Inc. All rights reserved.
© Photodisc
© Corbis Images

ISBN 1-59441-052-6

Table of Contents

About This Book 4

The Beads Go On (Making Jewelry) 5

Sorting, patterning, addition, subtraction, problem solving — 6-8

Join the PTA! (PTA Membership Drive) 9

Reading different kinds of graphs, problem solving, addition, subtraction — 10-12

Calendar Capers (Calendar) 13

Calendar skills, problem solving, addition — 14-16

What Did You Do at School? (School Schedule) 17

Time, schedules, problem solving, addition, subtraction — 18-20

Doughnuts for Dads (Boxes of Doughnuts) 21

Fractions, addition, subtraction, graphing, problem solving — 22-24

How's the Weather? (Weather Map) 25

Temperature, problem solving, subtraction, fractions — 26-28

Get Your Lemonade (Lemonade Stand) 29

Time, money, addition, subtraction, problem solving — 30-32

What's for Lunch? (Kids' Menu) 33

Money, addition, subtraction, problem solving — 34-36

Do Your Chores (Child's Chore List) 37

Money, problem solving, addition — 38-40

What Should I Wear? (Outfit Choices) 41

Problem solving, combinations, money, addition, subtraction — 42-44

Yummy Fruit Pizza (Recipe) 45

Addition, subtraction, fractions, following directions, problem solving — 46-48

Let's Go to the Movies (Movie Poster) 49

Schedules, time, money, problem solving, addition — 50-52

A Sweet Fund-Raiser (Bake Sale) 53

Problem solving, money, combinations, addition, subtraction — 54-56

Yard Sale Today (Yard Sale Items) 57

Money, addition, subtraction, problem solving, time — 58-60

Answer Key 61-64

About This Book...

Math is everywhere!

Real World Math was written to connect mathematics to real-world problems that students encounter in their daily lives. The activities in this book are designed to help students become independent problem solvers as they use patterns, elapsed time, calendars, measurement, money, and other mathematical concepts to solve problems.

The book contains 14 activities that focus on real-world problems. While using the picture at the beginning of each activity as a reference, students can demonstrate problem-solving skills by answering the questions on the following pages. Each picture is followed by two activity pages with short-answer and multiple-choice questions. The first activity page is geared toward lower-level thinking skills while the second activity page progresses through higher-level thinking. The two different formats allow you to differentiate how to use the activity for the varying learning levels of students.

A teacher notes and extensions section follows each activity. Each section includes a description of the picture that students will use to complete the worksheets. Review this description with students prior to having them complete the worksheets. The teacher notes contain teaching strategies and ideas for instruction. For example, The Beads Go On (page 8) has suggestions for teaching patterns to students learning the skill for the first time. Get Your Lemonade (page 32) suggests strategies for comparing money amounts, making change, and telling time. The teacher notes are designed to use as needed. In addition, theme-based extension activities are included. These activities are intended to give other options for expanding students' knowledge on the subject or providing cross-curricular connections. For example, Yard Sale Today (page 60) suggests a literature connection by having students read two different books with a yard sale theme. Learning the days of the week in Spanish and finding patterns on the calendar are extensions found in Calendar Capers (page 16). Using these ideas allows you to extend students' knowledge, as well as vary the activities according to students' needs.

As students use the activities in this book, they will begin to make more mathematical connections to the world in which they live. They will see that math truly is everywhere.

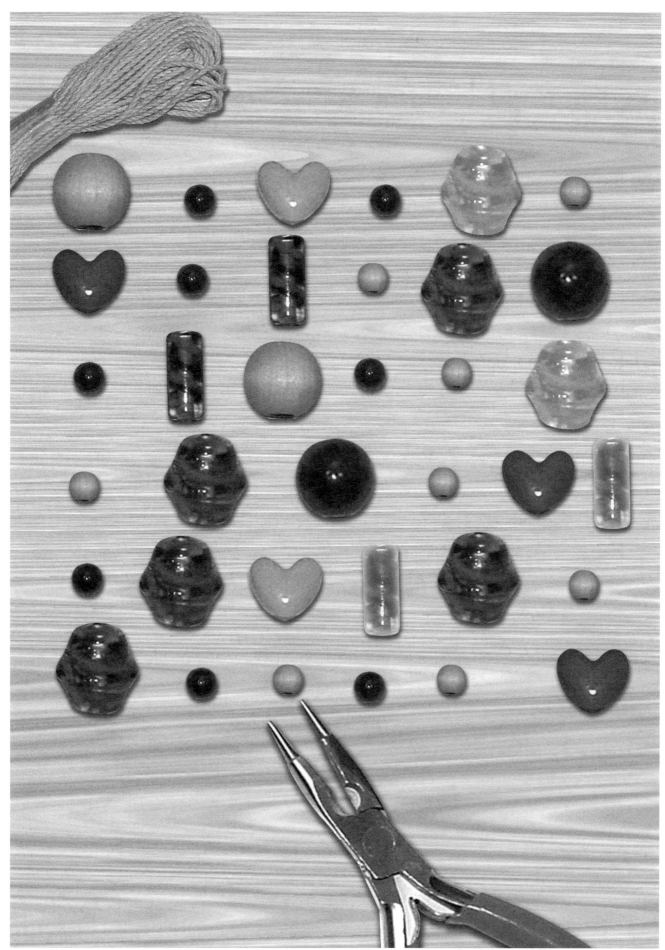

The Beads Go On

Use the different beads to answer the questions.

1. Jimmy counted the large beads. Megan counted the small beads. Who counted more beads?   _____

2. Which group has an odd number of beads?
    a. large, dark beads
    b. small, light beads
    c. heart-shaped beads   _____

3. How many beads are dark and round, but not large?   _____

4. Tara's teacher asks her to sort the beads by shape. How many groups will Tara make?   _____

5. Jenny made a bracelet for 50¢. She sold it for 75¢. How much money did she make?   _____

6. Caroline made a necklace that had an ABBC pattern. Draw a picture of what the necklace could look like.

The Beads Go On

Use the different beads to answer the questions.

1. How many dark beads would you need to take away to make the number of light beads and dark beads equal?

    _____

2. Rudy closed his eyes and picked a bead out of the bin. Which color is he more likely to have chosen?
    a. dark
    b. light

    _____

3. Sahid used all of the beads that are not round. How many dark beads did he use?

    _____

4. Brad took all of the small beads and Erin took all of the large beads. How many more beads did Erin take than Brad?

    _____

5. Hal shares all of the beads equally with his two friends. How many beads will each person get?

    _____

6. About how many beads are there total?
    a. 10
    b. 40
    c. 80

    _____

7. You have 30 cm of rope to make 3 necklaces of the same length. If bracelets are one-half the size of necklaces, how many bracelets can you make with the same amount of rope?

    _____

The Beads Go On

The Picture:

The beads on the table are used for making jewelry. In this lesson, they will be used to make necklaces and bracelets. The following beads are in the picture.

large, dark, round beads (2)
large, light, round beads (2)
small, dark, round beads (8)
small, light, round beads (8)
large, dark, hexagonal beads (5)
large, light, hexagonal beads (2)

large, dark, heart-shaped beads (3)
large, light, heart-shaped beads (2)
large, dark, cylindrical beads (2)
large, light, cylindrical beads (2)

Before having students complete the worksheets, discuss the color, shape, and size of the beads in the picture. Make sure students are successful at identifying the similarities and differences in the beads before creating their patterns. When showing possible pattern examples with the beads, use words like *dark, light, round, hexagonal, heart-shaped, small,* and *large.*

Teacher Notes:

When teaching students patterns, explain that there are many repeating patterns that are found in the real world. Calendars contain patterns in days of the week and months in a year. In counting, numbers in the ones place repeat every time the tens place increases.

There are different ways to identify patterns: by shape, by color, by size, by letters, or by numbers. These descriptions can be interchanged to rename patterns. For example, strawberry, banana, strawberry can be renamed red, yellow, red or ABA. The basic principle behind a pattern is "something that repeats." When introducing patterns to students, have them say the word *repeat* when they see the patterns starting over again.

Extension Activities:

1. Have students make jewelry for their mothers on Mother's Day. When they have completed their pieces of jewelry, have them describe what patterns they used, the shapes of the beads, and the length of the string they used.
2. Purchase colorful macaroni to use as beads for necklaces and bracelets.
3. Use hundreds board reproducibles to show patterns in numbers. Have students color numbers with even numbers in the ones place. Then, have students look for the patterns. Repeat this activity with different multiples to create different patterns.

CD-104023 • Real-World Math

Kindergarten

25
20
15
10
5

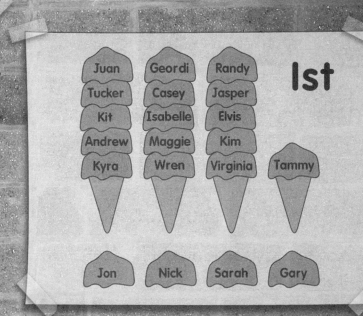

1st

Juan Geordi Randy
Tucker Casey Jasper
Kit Isabelle Elvis
Andrew Maggie Kim
Kyra Wren Virginia Tammy

Jon Nick Sarah Gary

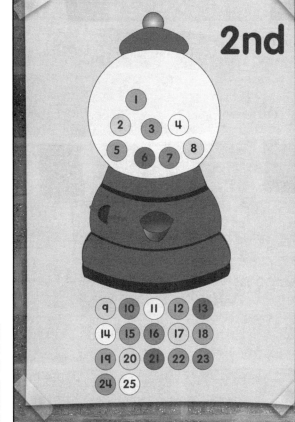

2nd

1
2 3 4
5 8
6 7

9 10 11 12 13
14 15 16 17 18
19 20 21 22 23
24 25

ALL OUR PARENTS

JOINED ___ ___

3rd

THE PTA

Join the PTA!

Use the PTA membership posters to answer the questions.

1. How many first-grade memberships have been sold? _____

2. On the first-grade poster, have Tammy's parents joined the PTA? _____

3. How many second graders need their parents to join to have 100% participation? _____

4. If it costs $2.00 to join the PTA, how much money have the first-grade parents paid? _____

5. Which class has a different number of students than the other 3 classes? _____

6. Have more third or first graders' parents joined the PTA? _____

7. The second grade had 5 more parents join the PTA. How many more parents need to join for them to reach their goal? _____

8. Which grade has sold the most memberships so far?
   a. kindergarten
   b. first grade
   c. second grade
   d. third grade _____

 CD-104023 • Real-World Math

Name _____

Join the PTA!

Use the PTA membership posters to answer the questions.

1. Isabelle has a brother who is 1 year older than
    she is. Which grade is her brother in?
    a. kindergarten
    b. first grade
    c. second grade
    d. third grade   _____

2. If half of the kindergarten students whose parents
    have joined the PTA are girls, how many girls
    are there?   _____

3. Add the number of students in first and third grades
    together. Is your answer even or odd?   _____

4. Which grade has the least number of students whose
    parents need to join the PTA?   _____

5. Including every grade level, how many parents have
    joined the PTA altogether?   _____

6. Which is greater, the number of first- and third-
    grade parents who joined the PTA, or the number
    of kindergarten and second-grade parents
    who joined the PTA?   _____

7. Principal Burcaw said that he would pay for all
    of the students whose parents have not joined
    the PTA. PTA membership costs $2.00. How much
    money does Mr. Burcaw have to pay?   _____

Join the PTA!

The Picture:

Each class has made a poster to show how many parents have joined the PTA.

- Kindergarten: A thermometer graph (bar graph) shows one line for every student's parents who have joined. The goal is 25 memberships.
- First grade: An ice cream scoop represents membership for each student's parents. A student's name moves from the bottom of the poster to the top of a cone when her parents join the PTA. The goal is 20 memberships.
- Second grade: A gum ball represents membership for each student's parents. As his parents join the PTA, a gum ball is taken from the bottom of the poster and placed inside the gum ball machine. The goal is 25 memberships.
- Third grade: Each letter of the phrase "All our parents joined the PTA" represents membership for each student's parents. Once a parent joins the PTA, the next letter is moved from the bottom of the page and placed on the next blank in the phrase. Third grade's membership goal is 25.

Teacher Notes:

Tell students that graphs are ways of showing information using pictures. The pictures stand for or represent something else. Graphs have two purposes: to organize information so that we can understand it and to present information in a useful way. By using different kinds of graphs, students can see that information can be represented in various ways.

Extension Activities:

1. Make a graph representing student attendance each day. Make a vertical list of students on a piece of poster board. Clip a clothespin to the right of each student's name. When a student enters the room for the day, have her move the clothespin to the left side of the poster board next to her name. Discuss with students how the graph shows information. All students with their clothespins on the left are present; all students with their clothespins on the right are absent. Explain to students that using a graph is a faster way of taking attendance because you only have to look at the right of the poster to see who is absent for the day.

2. Use a pictograph to show student preferences. Provide pictures of various objects with a common theme. For example, provide shapes of various fruits. Have students choose pictures of their favorite fruits. Draw an x-axis (horizontal) and y-axis (vertical) on the board. Number the y-axis and place a picture of each fruit below the x-axis. Have each student place a piece of tape on the back of his fruit picture, then place it directly above the matching fruit on the x-axis. Students should stack the pictures vertically until all students have placed their fruit on the graph. Discuss the information on the graph by asking students: Which was chosen most? Least? Did more than half choose one fruit?

3. Graph homework progress. Make a line graph representing students doing their homework for the week. Label the graph with Monday through Thursday on the x-axis and the number of students on the y-axis. Using numbers, not names, show how many students completed their homework each night. Set a goal of 100%!

February

Sunday	Monday	Tuesday	Wednesday	Thursday	Friday	Saturday
Celebrate Black History Month		1	2 Groundhog Day	3	4	5
6	7	8	9	10	11	12
13	14 Valentine's Day	15	16	17	18	19
20	21 Presidents' Day	22	23	24	25	26
27	28					

Name _____

Calendar Capers

Use the calendar to answer the questions.

1. On which day of the week is the first day
   of February?   _____

2. How many special days are in the month
   of February?   _____

3. Maya's first dance recital is the second Wednesday
   in February. What is the date of Maya's recital?   _____

4. Deacon's birthday is 2 weeks after Maya's dance
   recital. When is his birthday?   _____

5. Presidents' Day is February 21 and is a holiday.
   How many days of school will students have
   that week?   _____

6. Ling's aunt sent a postcard on Groundhog Day.
   She said that she would come next month to visit.
   In which month will Ling's aunt visit?   _____

7. Katie visits her grandmother on the third Saturday
   of every month. What date will she visit this month?   _____

8. Presidents' Day is in 2 weeks. What is today's date?   _____

Name _____

Calendar Capers

Use the calendar to answer the questions.

1. Tessa has piano lessons every Monday and Wednesday. How many lessons will she have in February?

    _____

2. If today's date is February 18, what day of the week was yesterday?

    _____

3. Richard wrote a report about Wilma Rudolph for Black History Month. It is due on the last Friday in February. What date is Richard's report due?

    _____

4. Susan bought valentine cards for her class on Saturday, February 5. How many days does she have to wait to give them to her friends?

    _____

5. Joe's birthday is on Valentine's Day. His best friend had a birthday party exactly 2 weeks earlier. What day of the week was his friend's party?

    _____

6. The summer Olympics are held every leap year. According to the calendar, will the summer Olympics be held this year?

    _____

7. Karen's sister was born 3 months before February 24. When was she born?

    _____

Calendar Capers

The Picture:

The picture is a calendar hanging on a refrigerator. It displays the month of February. Groundhog Day, Valentine's Day, and Presidents' Day are printed on the calendar.

Teacher Notes:

While most students know that calendars are used primarily to schedule events, show them the math in each calendar. When teaching calendar skills, point out the patterns in the calendar. The days of the week repeat every seven days, the months of the year repeat every 12 months. While the position of the first day of the month may shift from month to month, the dates will fall in a pattern based on the first date. For example, if February 1 is a Tuesday, February 8, 15, and 22 will also fall on Tuesdays. No matter what the month or the day of the week, the dates always fall in the same columns. Explain that to find the date of the same day of the next week, students should add seven to the date.

Teach students calendar vocabulary. Distinguish between the *day* (day of the week) and the *date* (a number). A *month* is approximately the amount of time it takes for the moon to travel around Earth. A *year* is the amount of time it takes Earth to travel around the sun. Every year, it takes 365 $\frac{1}{4}$ days for Earth to travel around the sun. The $\frac{1}{4}$ of a day each year is compounded into one day every four years. This is why every four years, February 29 is added to the calendar. This is called a *leap year*.

Extension Activities:

1. Give students 10 minutes to write different ways to use a calendar. Some examples might be the monthly school lunch menu, after-school activities, sporting events, birthdays, holidays, etc. After 10 minutes, have students exchange papers. Go around the room and have each student name something from the list. Write each named item on the board or overhead projector. If another student has the same item on his list, he should cross it off. After all students have had turns, the student with the most items remaining on her list wins a prize. Talk about all of the items students listed. Play again by asking places you would find a calendar or people who use calendars every day.
2. Turn the days of the week into math problems. At the beginning of math, ask a student today's date. Once the student has given a correct answer, have students write math riddles or number sentences that have the date as their answers. For example, if the date is the third, then students could write "9 - 6" or "the number of sides on a triangle."
3. Write the date on the board with students in the room. This is a great opportunity to get students involved! Students can help you spell the day of the week and the month. They can use their logical thinking skills by saying "Yesterday was ___, so today is ___."
4. Learn the days of the week and months of the year in Spanish.

School Day Schedule

Time	Activity
8:00 - 10:00	Reading
10:00 - 12:00	Mathematics
12:00 - 12:30	Lunch
12:30 - 1:00	Recess
1:00 - 2:00	Enrichment Class (See schedule.)
2:00 - 3:00	Science

Enrichment Class Schedule

Day	Class/Teacher
Monday	Media Center Mrs. Hagborg
Tuesday	Art Mr. Beard
Wednesday	Music Mrs. Matthews
Thursday	Physical Education Mrs. Brown
Friday	Spanish Señor Almeida

After-School Schedule

Day/Time	Activity/Location
Monday 3:00 - 4:00	Book Club Media Center
Tuesday 3:00 - 4:30	Science Club Science Lab
Wednesday 3:00 - 4:30	Math Club Room 22
Wednesday 3:00 - 4:00	Spelling Bee Club Media Center
Thursday 3:00 - 3:30	Chess Club Room 14
Monday - Friday 3:00 - 6:00	After-School Care Gymnasium

What Did You Do at School?

Use the schedules to answer the questions.

1. Kaleb is great at adding and subtracting. What after-school club should he join? _____

2. Cara left school at the end of recess for a dentist appointment. What time did she leave school? _____

3. The principal walked in Mrs. Hatfield's class when math class started. What time did the principal come in the room? _____

4. Roger's mother picked him up after Chess Club. Where did she go to pick him up? _____

5. Leigh's favorite enrichment class is on Tuesday. Which is her favorite? _____

6. What time is school over for the day?
   a. 12:00
   b. 2:00
   c. 3:00
   d. 6:00 _____

7. How long does the Spelling Bee Club meet? _____

What Did You Do at School?

Use the schedules to answer the questions.

1. Which of the after-school activities lasts the least amount of time? _____

2. Ahmad stays on Friday until 4:15 at after-school care. He has 45 minutes of homework to do. How many minutes of free time will he have before he leaves? _____

3. Mrs. Brown does stretching for the first half of P. E. class. How long does she do stretching? _____

4. Wayne went to the Science Club, then he went to after-school care until 5:30. How long was he in after-school care? _____

5. Fiona was absent from class during reading and mathematics. How many hours of school did she miss? _____

6. Megan stays after school for Book Club and Math Club. How many hours does she stay after school each week? _____

What Did You Do at School?

The Picture:

The picture is schedules hanging on a bulletin board in a classroom. The three different schedules listed are for the school day, enrichment classes, and after-school activities. The schedules give different information. The Enrichment Schedule tells the day of the week, name of the class, and teacher for each enrichment class. The School Day Schedule names the activities of the school day and the time period for each. The After-School Schedule lists different activities, the locations of the activities, and the time and day of each activity.

Teacher Notes:

Schedules can be used for various reasons. Explain to students that some schedules stay the same over time while others may change. Jobs, sporting events, airplanes, and even doctors depend on schedules. Schedules keep things running on time so that people can plan how to use the time in each day, week, month, or year. When teaching students a schedule that includes time in a day, it is best to use a clock with hands that advance the hour as the minute hand advances. Introduce the term *elapsed time* to teach students about time that has gone by. Explain that elapsed time can be determined by counting the minutes or hours from a starting time to an ending time. If there are minutes and hours to calculate, students should count the number of minutes from the starting point to the next hour, then count the remaining number of hours. If there are more minutes after the hour, calculate them separately. Have students add the minutes and hours together to get total time. For example, to calculate elapsed time from 4:32-6:17, first find the number of minutes from 4:32-5:00 (28 minutes). Then, count the hours from 5:00-6:00 (1 hour). Finally, find the remaining minutes from 6:00-6:17 (17 minutes). The total elapsed time is 1 hour and 45 minutes.

Extension Activities:

1. Have students practice elapsed time by using manipulative clocks with hour hands that advance as the minute hands advance. Give students specific activities that happen within the school day, such as lunch or recess. Have them count how many times the minute hand crosses over the 12 to count the hours that will elapse. Begin with times that start and end on the hour, then slowly progress to times that include the half hour.

2. Have students keep track of their daily schedules. Have them write the things they do on a specific day. They should include starting and ending times on their schedules. Ask if they can figure out how much time they spend doing each activity. To extend this activity, have students keep track of their schedules for a week. Have them compare how the schedules change each day.

3. Speed things up! Keep track of how long it takes for students to do simple things in the classroom, such as line up for lunch, unpack their book bags, or line up for recess. Using a clock with a second hand or a stopwatch, see how long it takes students to do each activity and see if they can improve the time each day. At the end of the week, talk to students about what made things go faster or what obstacles made them go slower.

4. Have students come up with some after-school clubs for their school. Then, have students create a schedule with the information. If your school already has several activities, gather the information and have students make one schedule for all of the clubs.

Welcome to Doughnuts for Dads

Name _____

Doughnuts for Dads

Use the boxes of doughnuts to answer the questions.

1. Miss Taylor sent notes home to ask how many dads would like to come to the doughnut breakfast. The dads were also asked which 2 doughnut flavors they would like to eat. As the dads sent in their answers, Miss Taylor made a graph so that she would know which doughnuts to buy. Refer to the boxes of doughnuts as you fill in the graph below to show what Miss Taylor bought.

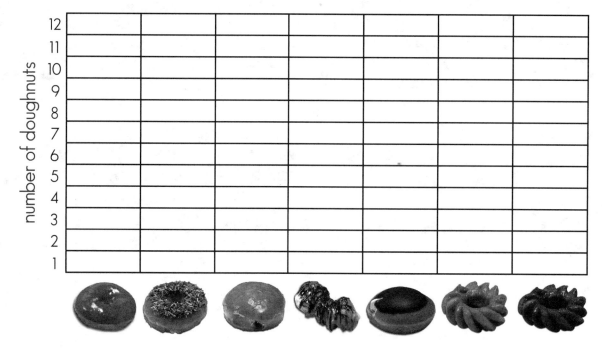

2. Danny's dad ate 2 plain doughnuts. How many plain doughnuts were left? _____

3. Which is greater, the number of doughnuts with center holes or without center holes? _____

CD-104023 • Real-World Math

Doughnuts for Dads

Use the boxes of doughnuts to answer the questions.

1. Steven's dad and Bill's dad ate all of the plain doughnuts. What fraction of the doughnuts did they eat?

    _____

2. If 12 dads shared half of the doughnuts equally, how many did each dad eat?

    _____

3. Bob chose a doughnut from the box with jelly doughnuts and doughnuts with sprinkles. What is the chance he chose a doughnut with sprinkles?

    _____

4. Miss Taylor bought all of the doughnuts for the breakfast. How many doughnuts did she buy?

    _____

5. Miss Taylor bought enough doughnuts so that each person would have 2. How many people was Miss Taylor expecting to come to the breakfast?

    _____

6. There were 7 doughnuts left at the end of the breakfast. How many doughnuts were eaten?

    _____

Doughnuts for Dads

The Picture:
There are 12 doughnuts in each of the four boxes on the table.
Top, left: 8 cream filled with chocolate frosting, 4 chocolate twists
Top, right: 12 plain doughnuts
Bottom, left: 6 sprinkle doughnuts, 6 jelly doughnuts
Bottom, right: 8 chocolate crullers, 4 plain crullers

Teacher Notes:
Describe each of the doughnuts to students and teach them the name for each.

Teach students about the word *dozen*. Doughnuts, eggs in a carton, and roses come by the dozen. Discuss with students other things that come in groups of 12.

Fractions, such as $\frac{1}{2}$, $\frac{1}{3}$, and $\frac{2}{3}$, can be taught with doughnuts! Fractions are part of a group, so discuss how many of one kind of doughnut are in each box. The number in the denominator is the total number of doughnuts in the box. The number in the numerator would be the portion of the total that are grouped together. For example, there are six sprinkle doughnuts and six jelly doughnuts in a box. If there are 12 doughnuts all together, $\frac{6}{12}$ of the doughnuts have sprinkles. Or, ask, "How many different kinds of doughnuts are in the box?" Two, sprinkles and jelly. Of the two different kinds of doughnuts, $\frac{1}{2}$ are sprinkles and $\frac{1}{2}$ are jelly.

Teach directional terms, such as *left, right, above, below*, and *beside*, to distinguish between the boxes.

Extension Activities:
1. Hold a special breakfast in the classroom for parents and guardians. Have students write invitations asking their parents or guardians to attend. Make sure to include an RSVP line and ask them to choose their favorite doughnut flavors. When all invitations have been returned, have students graph the different types of doughnuts and estimate the numbers of doughnuts they will need from the RSVPs that were returned.
2. Make cinnamon doughnuts in class. Cut canned biscuits into quarters. Remind students that $\frac{1}{4}$ is a fraction. Place the dough in an electric deep fryer for two minutes until they are golden brown. Allow students to count the time using a second hand on a clock. Remove from oil with a metal basket or tongs. Let students help roll the doughnuts in one part cinnamon, two parts sugar combined. Review ratios while they do this. Allow doughnuts to cool and let students eat for a snack. (Before completing any food activity, ask families' permission and inquire about students' food allergies and religious or other food preferences.)
3. Have students categorize the doughnuts. Possible categories could be plain, chocolate dough, frosting, sprinkles, filling, or hole in the center. Then, let students use the information to create a Venn diagram.

THE WEATH

TERRIFIC 5-DAY FORECAST

Monday	Tuesday	Wednesday	Thursday	Friday
80°F/27°C	88°F/31°C	90°F/32°C	92°F/33°C	95°F/35°C
69°F/20°C	69°F/20°C	70°F/21°C	73°F/23°C	

NATION

| 40s | 50s | 60s | 70s | 80s | 90s | 100s |

Seattle
68°F/51°F

Portland
77°F/61°F

Billings
83°F/70°F

Minneapolis
68°F/47°F

Boston
69°F/52°F

Boise
92°F/67°F

Detroit
70°F/52°F

New York
72°F/50°F

San Francisco
66°F/51°F

Salt Lake City
90°F/63°F

Omaha
85°F/72°F

Chicago
73°F/50°F

Cincinnati
75°F/53°F

Denver
83°F/59°F

St. Louis
87°F/73°F

Nashville
89°F/75°F

Las Vegas
102°F/81°F

Los Angeles
74°F/62°F

Phoenix
104°F/83°F

Atlanta
94°F/76°F

Dallas
89°F/75°F

Houston
91°F/75°F

New Orleans
90°F/73°F

Tampa
91°F/75°F

Miami
92°F/75°F

SUNRISE 6:38 A.M.
SUNSET 8:09 P.M.

N
W   E
S

How's the Weather?

Use the weather map to answer the questions.

1. How much hotter is it supposed to be in Houston today than in New Orleans? _____

2. How many days of the week are not shown on the forecast? _____

3. Roger's bedtime is 9 minutes before the sun sets. What time is Roger's bedtime? _____

4. Which day will be hotter, Tuesday or Friday? _____

5. How many days on the 5-day forecast are supposed to be sunny?
   a. 1
   b. 2
   c. 4
   d. 5 _____

6. If the high on Monday is 80°F, how many degrees hotter will it get on Tuesday?
   a. 2
   b. 8
   c. 88
   d. 92 _____

7. Which city will be the coldest? _____

How's the Weather?

Use the weather map to answer the questions.

1. What fraction of the days on the 5-day forecast
    are supposed to be rainy?

    _____

2. Jenny lives in Atlanta. She is going to visit her
    friend in Miami. What is the difference between
    the high temperatures in the 2 cities?

    _____

    a. 4°F
    b. 1°F
    c. 5°F
    d. 2°F

    _____

3. The low temperature on Wednesday night
    will be 70°F/21°C. How many °F will the
    temperature have risen by the time it reaches
    the high temperature on Thursday?

    _____

    How many °C will the temperature rise?

    _____

4. What is the difference between the high
    temperature and the low temperature
    on Tuesday in °F?

    _____

    What is the difference in °C?

    _____

5. Anna leaves for camp at 7:30 A.M. If she gets
    out of bed at sunrise, how long does she have
    to get ready to leave?

    _____

How's the Weather?

The Picture:

The picture is a weather map from a newspaper called *Terrific Times*. The temperatures shown are in Fahrenheit and Celsius. The high temperature for each day is listed under the picture of the weather conditions. The lows for the evenings are listed between the days of the week. The national weather map lists certain cities and their highs and lows in degrees Fahrenheit. The color-coding system shows dark areas for high temperatures and light areas for low temperatures throughout the country.

Teacher Notes:

Tell students that people rely on weather forecasts when they make plans for the day and even the week. Weather reports also let people know when they need to water their plants and help them decide what clothes to wear. Many people rely on weather reports to do their jobs. For example, farmers rely on the weather for good crops, and people who work on computers watch for days where heavy lightning can zap computers!

People who predict the weather are called *meteorologists*. They use computers and mathematical equations to predict the weather.

Extension Activities:

1. Talk about different kinds of storms and which areas are most affected. For example, the U.S. states of Louisiana, Arkansas, Missouri, Nebraska, Texas, Kansas, and Oklahoma and the Canadian province of New Brunswick are known to have hundreds of tornadoes every year. These storms are tracked by storm chasers who use mathematical equations to determine where the next storm will be. They also use this information to warn people that a tornado is coming. Snowstorms are common in the northern U.S. states, while in parts of Florida people wear swimsuits in December!
2. Talk about what weather conditions are best for certain activities. Then, have students draw pictures of themselves participating in fun outdoor activities and write what the temperature would be outside for those activities.
3. Have a meteorologist come to your school or visit a weather center in your area on a field trip.
4. Chart the weather for one month in your classroom. See if you find any patterns in the weather throughout the month.
5. Search the Internet to find out the times the sun will rise and set in your area. Create a graph to show how days become shorter from fall to winter and longer from winter to spring. Even though all days have 24 hours, the amount of daylight changes every day, making the days appear longer or shorter. Have students create a bar graph and ask if they notice a pattern. Ask if there are days in spring and fall with the same amount of daylight.

Fresh-Squeezed Lemonade
Today 12:00-2:00

Large (20 oz.) – 25¢
Medium (10 oz.) – 15¢
Small (5 oz.) – 10¢

Get Your Lemonade

Use the lemonade stand to answer the questions.

1. Mr. Wilson asks for a 10 oz. lemonade. Which size
    did Mr. Wilson order?
    a. small
    b. medium
    c. large   _____

2. How many hours is the lemonade stand open?   _____

3. How many more ounces are in a large than
    a small?   _____

4. It takes 15 minutes to clean up the lemonade stand.
    What time did Sid and Sara finish?   _____

5. It takes 1 lemon to make a 5 oz. lemonade. How many
    lemons does it take to make 2 10 oz. lemonades?   _____

6. Ricky ordered 2 large lemonades and 1 small
    lemonade. How much did Ricky pay?
    a. 35¢
    b. 40¢
    c. 50¢
    d. 60¢   _____

7. How many small lemonades do you need to equal
    1 large lemonade?   _____

8. Jenny paid for her lemonade with 1 dime, 2 nickels,
    and 5 pennies. What size did she buy?   _____

Get Your Lemonade

Use the lemonade stand to answer the questions.

1. Larry and Louise shared 1 large and 1 medium lemonade. How many ounces did they each drink? _____

2. Missy spent 35¢ to buy 2 drinks. What size drinks did she buy? _____

3. Gavin has to buy lemonade for his 4 brothers. If he only has 50¢, what size should he buy so that each brother can have his own lemonade? _____

4. You have 1 quarter, 1 dime, and 2 nickels. Can you buy 2 large drinks? _____

5. Randy paid for his lemonade with a quarter. He got 10¢ change. What size did Randy buy?
   a. small
   b. medium
   c. large _____

6. One pitcher holds 60 oz. of lemonade.

   How many large cups are in one pitcher? _____

   How many medium cups are in one pitcher? _____

   How many small cups are in one pitcher? _____

Get Your Lemonade

The Picture:
The picture is a lemonade stand. It has a sign that gives the hours of operation, the sizes of the drinks, and the prices.

Teacher Notes:
Tell students that there are many ways that children can earn money. One way is to sell lemonade on a hot day. Teaching students about money is an important skill. With a lemonade stand, students learn the concept of cost versus profit, as well as how to count money and make change.

When teaching students to count change, have them count coins to the nearest 10 and "count up" to the next coin. For example, if a person gives a student a quarter for a cup of lemonade that is 10¢, the student can add a dime to get to the next 10 (20¢) and then add a nickel to equal 25¢. Students using this method can exchange multiple coins for single coins of the same value. If a student using the counting up method adds three nickels to count up from 10¢ to 25¢, have her practice exchanging two nickels for a dime.

When teaching students to compute standard time, show them that there is a pattern. Explain that beginning at midnight, the clock goes through its first cycle of the pattern from 12:00 A.M. (midnight) to 11:59 A.M. The pattern begins again with 12:00 P.M. at noon. Show that 12:00 noon becomes a starting point for counting hours and can be substituted with a zero to make counting easier.

Extension Activities:
1. Have students talk about times when a lemonade stand would make the most money. What location should they choose? What should the weather be like? What slogan can they use to make people want to try their lemonade? Are there any bicycle or running races where many hot, thirsty people will be present?
2. Discuss with students how a lemonade stand works. Have students brainstorm about how much money must be spent before the stand can open and what items need to be purchased in advance. Have students make a list of the supplies needed to open their own lemonade stands.
3. Make lemonade with students. Purchase or have parents donate fresh lemons, sugar, a carton of prepared lemonade, a can of frozen lemonade, and a container of powdered lemonade. Make one pitcher of each type of lemonade. Keep the receipts from the purchases to talk about the cost of each pitcher. Have students conduct a taste test of the different lemonade and choose a favorite. Discuss the advantages and disadvantages of the products purchased for each type of lemonade. (Before completing any food activity, ask families' permission and inquire about students' food allergies and religious or other food preferences.)

The Redbird Café Kids' Menu

Food on this menu is for children ages 10 and under.

Grilled Cheese Sandwich....$1.95
- Cheddar or American cheese

Cheeseburger $2.15
- Served with ketchup

Chicken Strips $2.25
- Served with ranch or honey mustard sauce

Hot Dog..............$1.00
- Served with ketchup

Hamburger..........$2.00
- Served with ketchup

Spaghetti..............$2.25
- Served with garlic bread

Tacos $2.00
- Two beef tacos topped with cheese and lettuce

All children's meals are served with milk and carrot sticks.

French fries are 50¢ extra.

What's for Lunch?

Use the menu to answer the questions.

1. How many different food items can you choose from on the Kids' Menu?

   _____

2. How many items are served with ketchup?

   _____

3. Which item on the Kids' Menu cost one dollar and ninety-five cents?

   _____

4. How much more is a cheeseburger than a hamburger?

   _____

5. Which item on the Kids' Menu costs the least amount of money?

   _____

6. Kareem wants a hot dog and french fries. How much will his order cost?

   _____

7. Ravi's mom ordered lunch for him. She asked if he wanted ranch or honey mustard. What did Ravi's mom order?

   _____

8. Shaniqua ordered the tacos. Her sister ordered a hot dog. How much was lunch for both of them?
   a. $1.00
   b. $2.00
   c. $3.00

   _____

What's for Lunch?

Use the menu to answer the questions.

1. All 5 of Mrs. Smith's children order french fries with their meals. If just the meals cost $9.15, how much more will the total be?

   _____

2. How many menu items have cheese?

   _____

3. How much does it cost to get 1 order of tacos and 2 orders of spaghetti?

   _____

4. Steven ordered a hot dog. If he has a 1 dollar bill, 2 dimes, and 1 quarter, can he get an order of french fries?

   _____

5. Jamie and Rick share an order of tacos with a side of french fries. How much does each of them need to pay?

   _____

6. Which of the following is the least expensive?
   a. tacos
   b. chicken strips
   c. cheeseburger
   d. grilled cheese sandwich with french fries

   _____

7. Mom paid with a $5.00 bill for Jane and Sarah. She got 50¢ change. What did they order from the menu?
   a. spaghetti and chicken strips
   b. hot dog and tacos
   c. grilled cheese sandwich and spaghetti

   _____

What's for Lunch?

The Picture:

The picture is a kids' menu from a restaurant. Children who are 10 years old and younger can order from the kids' menu. There are seven different menu items, and each item is served with milk and carrot sticks. French fries can be added to each menu item for an additional 50¢.

Teacher Notes:

Menus are a great way to teach about money, combinations, and choices. Using coin and bill manipulatives, help students in the beginning stages of counting money and making change. Talk about the different monetary value of each coin and bill and the number of coins and bills it takes to make equivalent amounts.

When teaching students about money, one of the most important skills is lining up the decimal points before adding or subtracting. Demonstrate these skills as a group before giving the reproducibles to students. First, have students practice stacking money amounts rather than writing horizontal number sentences. Practice by writing the decimal point first, then write the correct dollar value to the left of the decimal point and the change amount to the right of the decimal point. Talk students through this process each time you write a money value. Have them repeat the process as you write the problems on the board. If you are adding two amounts together or subtracting one amount from another, follow the same process by writing the second decimal point directly below the decimal point of the first value.

Extension Activities:

1. Bring in various kids' menus from different restaurants and display them on a bulletin board. Have students choose their favorite meals from the restaurants and graph the results.
2. Using the different restaurant menus from the previous activity, have students see which menu items the different restaurants have in common. Have students give reasons why different restaurants offer the same menu items.
3. Have each student create a kids' menu. Students can name the restaurants and choose what items they would like to include on the kids' menus.
4. Teach combinations by discussing hamburgers or hot dogs with different topping choices. For example, if a plain hamburger has lettuce, tomatoes, and pickles as topping choices, that allows for a variety of combinations. Have students brainstorm all of the possible combinations.

    *   plain hamburger
    *   hamburger with lettuce
    *   hamburger with tomato
    *   hamburger with pickles
    *   hamburger with lettuce and tomato
    *   hamburger with lettuce and pickles
    *   hamburger with tomato and pickles
    *   hamburger with lettuce, tomato, and pickles

Do Your Chores

Use the chore list to answer the questions.

1. How many different chores are on the chore list for this week?   _____

2. Which chore pays the most money?   _____

3. If Kennedy sets the table every night this week for dinner and once for breakfast, how much will she earn?   _____

4. Dean emptied the wastepaper baskets 2 times this week. How much money did he earn?   _____

5. Haily earned $3.00 after doing 2 chores. Which 2 chores did she do?
   a. Sweep the kitchen and help wash the car.
   b. Help wash the car and rake leaves in the front yard.
   c. Rake leaves in the front yard and help put away groceries.   _____

6. Adam swept the kitchen 2 times and bundled the newspapers once. How much money did he earn this week?   _____

7. Lamar set the table and emptied the wastepaper baskets. Lauren helped wash the car. Who made more money?   _____

Do Your Chores

Use the chore list to answer the questions.

1. Mike earned 50¢ on Wednesday doing 1 chore.
   Which chore did he do?
   a. Bundle newspapers and set the table.
   b. Help wash the car.
   c. Sweep the kitchen.   _____

2. Heather did all of the chores she could do outside.
   How much money did Heather earn for doing
   her chores?   _____

3. Nelson set the table every night this week except
   Monday. How much money did he earn?   _____

4. Carrie saved $3.00 from sweeping the kitchen
   this month. How many times did she do her chore
   this month?   _____

5. Robert did all of the chores on the list. How much
   money did he earn if he did each chore once?   _____

6. Wendy received 1 dollar for doing a chore twice
   in 1 week. Which chore did Wendy do twice?   _____
   a. Help wash the car.
   b. Set the table.
   c. Set the table and empty the wastepaper baskets.
   d. Help put away groceries.

7. Matt raked leaves 4 times this month. Beth washed
   the car 6 times this month. Who earned more money
   this month?   _____

Do Your Chores

The Picture:

The picture is a list of children's chores. There is an amount next to each chore that will be paid after each chore is completed. Some chores may be completed several times during the week while others, such as helping to wash the car, may only need to be completed once during the week.

Teacher Notes:

Teach math vocabulary associated with money. Describe the difference between the following terms:

- coins and dollar bills
- receiving money and earning money
- spending money and saving money

- borrowing money and lending money
- money well spent and wasting money
- cash, checks, and credit

Have a discussion with students about how the amounts for some of the chores are different. The chores with higher dollar values require a child to do activities that take longer amounts of time and require more physical effort. Chores with lower values assigned to them can be done quickly and without much effort. The benefit of the lower value chores is that they can be performed several times throughout the week to accumulate more money. For example, if a child sets the table every night during the week, she can earn $1.75 with little effort.

Extension Activities:

1. Hold a job fair in your classroom. Send home a questionnaire for parents or guardians to fill out. Students can present the information, or parents can volunteer to come in to talk about their jobs. Include the following categories on the questionnaire:

    - name of your job
    - responsibilities
    - number of hours a week you work
    - payment type—salary, tips, by the hour, etc.

    - working environment—office, home, store, etc.
    - education needed for the job
    - best part of your job
    - worst part of your job

2. Discuss with students different ways they might be able to receive money. Some students may do chores, some may have lemonade stands, and others may receive money as gifts. Make a list of ways that students can earn money.

3. Discuss with students the value of saving money. Have students set goals for items they would like to buy. Have students estimate how long it will take to achieve their goals and explain how they came up with their estimates. Talk about what types of things they will do to earn money and achieve their goals.

Name _____

What Should I Wear?

Use the doll clothes to answer the questions.

1. How many boxes of clothes have stripes?   _____

2. If you buy the box with the pants that convert
    to shorts, how many different outfits can you make?   _____

3. Cindy has $4.00 to spend on doll clothes. What
    is the most number of boxes she can buy?   _____

4. Jacob bought his cousin the outfit with the pants
    that convert to shorts. If he paid with a $5.00 bill,
    what was his change?   _____

5. Monica is saving her money to buy the box
    of clothes with the short-sleeved, striped shirt.
    She has saved $1.00. How much more money does
    she need?
    a. 50¢
    b. $1.00
    c. $2.00   _____

6. Tina wants to buy the box with the skirt. She has
    6 quarters. She borrowed the rest from her brother.
    How much money did she borrow?   _____

CD-104023 • Real-World Math

Name _____

What Should I Wear?

Use the doll clothes to answer the questions.

1. The salesperson at the store forgot to put a price tag on one box. Each box with one outfit is $2.00, and each box that makes two outfits is $3.00. What price should she put on the box with the missing price tag?

    _____

2. Timothy has $4.00 to spend on a gift to donate to the school toy drive. If he spends all of his money, how many outfits can he buy?

    _____

3. Betsy wanted to buy all 4 boxes of clothes for her doll. How much money does Betsy need?

    _____

4. Leslie wants an outfit with a striped skirt and a white shirt. She will need to buy two boxes. Can she get what she wants for $4.00?

    _____

5. Donna is saving her allowance to buy the box of Bonnie clothes with the pants that convert to shorts. She has saved $2.75 so far. How much more money does she need to buy the box of clothes?

    _____

6. Mrs. Zorn bought the box with the skirt and the box with the short-sleeved, striped shirt. How many different outfits can be made with these 2 boxes?
    a. one
    b. two
    c. three
    d. four

    _____

What Should I Wear?

The Picture:
The picture is a display of four different boxes of doll clothes. The two boxes on top each contain one outfit. The box on the bottom left can make two different outfits because the pants can become shorts. The outfit on the bottom right can also make two different outfits and is missing a price tag.

Teacher Notes:
Clothes are a great way to teach combinations. Explain that people wear different combinations of clothes. Demonstrate how to make possible combinations by making lists. Starting with one box of clothes, have students list all of the possible combinations. For example, using the box with the white shorts, have students list the possible outfit combinations with the two shirts.
- white shorts and long-sleeved, striped shirt
- white shorts and short-sleeved, black shirt

Extension Activities:
1. Cut out pictures of clothes from a catalog or store advertisement. Make sure each student has pictures of at least two shirts and two pairs of pants, shorts, or skirts. Have students use the pictures as manipulatives and make lists of the different outfits they can make. After they have completed the lists, have them glue the pictures of the clothes to the lists.
2. Have a fashion show! Have students stand at the front of the room and talk about the outfits they are wearing. Ask if there are combinations of clothes from different students that can be worn together. Talk about the combinations and describe how each piece of clothing can make a different combination.
3. Discuss different ways to find out how much the box of clothes that is missing a price tag costs.
   - Explain that many stores have scanners that determine prices from bar codes even if there is not a price tag on an item. Show some product bar codes and explain how they are different.
   - Compare the box with other boxes that have similar products. The box without a price has two possible outfit combinations. The other box with two possible outfit combinations is $3.00, so there is a possibility that the box without a price tag costs the same.
   - Take two outfits to a cashier. Once the cashier gives the total price, subtract the price you know to determine the price you don't know.
4. Discuss getting more for your money. There are two boxes that each contain one outfit for $2.00. The other two boxes each contain two outfits for $3.00. The boxes with two outfits are a better value.

Fruit Pizza

Ingredients:
- 1 can of sugar cookie dough
- 1 8-ounce (225 g) package of cream cheese
- $\frac{1}{2}$ cup powdered sugar
- 3 cups of cut fruit (strawberries, blueberries, raspberries, oranges, cherries, kiwi)

Directions:
1. Preheat oven to 375°F (190°C).
2. Take cream cheese out of refrigerator to soften.
3. Roll cookie dough with a rolling pin until it is flat and place it on a round cookie sheet.
4. Bake for 10 minutes, then let it cool.
5. Mix cream cheese and sugar together.
6. Spread cream cheese mixture on cookie crust.
7. Put pieces of fruit on top.
8. Cut into wedges before serving.

Each pizza makes 8 servings.

Nutritional Facts per Serving: calories 200, total fat 10 g

Veggie Delight Pizza (See recipe on opposite page.)

Yummy Fruit Pizza

Use the fruit pizza recipe to answer the questions.

1. How many different kinds of fruit are in the fruit pizza recipe?

   _____

2. Carrie just finished step 4. What fraction shows how many steps she has done?

   a. $\frac{3}{8}$

   b. $\frac{4}{8}$

   c. $\frac{5}{8}$

   d. $\frac{8}{8}$

   _____

3. Theresa let the dough cook for 7 minutes. How many more minutes does the dough need?

   _____

4. Kelly's mom bought a package of cream cheese that is 225 grams. How many ounces is that?

   _____

5. Ann covered $\frac{3}{4}$ of her pizza with fruit. How many servings did not have fruit?

   _____

6. The oven was set at 375°F. How many degrees Celsius is that?

   _____

7. Joe wanted to eat 2 servings of the fruit pizza when it was finished. How many servings would be left?

   _____

Yummy Fruit Pizza

Use the fruit pizza recipe to answer the questions.

1. Zachary ate 3 servings of fruit pizza. How many
    calories are in 3 servings of fruit pizza?   _____

2. How many servings would be in 4 fruit pizzas?   _____

3. Johan is making 2 pizzas for his class. How much
    powdered sugar will he need for 2 pizzas?   _____

4. How many grams of fat are in the whole fruit pizza?   _____

5. Olivia bought 24 ounces (675 g) of cream cheese
    to make fruit pizza. How many pizzas is she planning
    to make?   _____

6. Mom wanted to bake 4 fruit pizzas for her aunt's
    party. How many cups of powdered sugar will
    she need?   _____

7. Sam's oven is too hot. If the oven reads 425°F, how
    many degrees does the oven have to cool before
    Sam can bake the dough?   _____

Yummy Fruit Pizza

The Picture:

The picture is a page from a cookbook. The recipe is for fruit pizza. The ingredients, step-by-step directions, number of servings, and number of calories and grams of fat are also included.

Teacher Notes:

Teach students about the measuring cup and tablespoon used in cooking. Using these special cooking tools ensures that all of the ingredients are measured the same way every time a recipe is made.

Pose the problem of doubling the recipe to make more fruit pizza. Ask students how they might solve this problem. Present the idea of using the doubles strategy.

Customary Measurement:
2 tablespoons + 2 tablespoons = 4 tablespoons
2 + 2 = 4
Double 2 = 4

Metric Measurement:
5 mL + 5 mL = 10 mL
5 + 5 = 10
Double 5 = 10

Students may have difficulty with the $1/2$-cup measurement. Explain to students that when something is cut in half, it has two halves. Therefore, two halves make a whole.

Extension Activities:

1. Provide a variety of kitchen measurement tools for students. Let students determine equivalent measures using sand or dried rice. For example:
    - 3 teaspoons = 1 tablespoon
    - 4 tablespoons = $1/4$ cup
    - 16 tablespoons = 1 cup
2. Create a class cookbook. Have students bring in their favorite family recipes. Then, have students categorize the different courses and types of food. Make copies of all of the recipes and send the cookbooks home with students.
3. Make a fruit pizza for the class. Decorate the pizza by making a pattern with the fruit. Have students identify the pattern using an ABC or 123 renaming strategy. (Before completing any food activity, ask families' permission and inquire about students' food allergies and religious or other food preferences.)
4. Introduce equivalent fractions when cutting a "pizza" made of paper. Using different-colored paper cut into congruent circles, show students how to make fractions, such as $1/2$, $1/4$, $1/8$, and $1/16$.

JOHNNY SAILOR
IN

Pirates of the Lost Islands

large popcorn $3.00
medium popcorn $2.50
small popcorn $2.25
sodas $1.50
*Combo: soda &
med. popcorn $3.75

SPECIAL SCHOOL DISCOUNTS
First 50 students
per school admitted free.
Each additional ticket $2.00.
No charge for teachers.

Show Times:
8:00 A.M., 10:00 A.M., 12:00 P.M.

Name _____

Let's Go to the Movies

Use the movie poster to answer the questions.

1. What time does the earliest movie begin? _____

2. Sally is getting ready to go to the movies with her mom. If it is 10:00 A.M. now, how many hours will it be until the next show? _____

3. Tom bought a medium popcorn. Nancy bought a large popcorn. How much more was Nancy's popcorn? _____

4. Lizzie spent $2.50. What did she buy? _____

5. There are 60 students in the first grade. How many will have to pay for tickets? _____

   How much will all of the extra tickets cost? _____

6. Five students order large popcorns. How much will their popcorns cost altogether? _____

7. Debbie's school is 20 minutes from the theater. Her class left school at 9:30 A.M. to go to the movie. Which show time are they going to see? _____

Let's Go to the Movies

Use the movie poster to answer the questions.

1. How much money will you save if you buy the combo?   _____

2. How much will it cost to buy 4 small popcorns and 4 sodas?   _____

3. Justin's mom gave him $2.50 to buy a box of popcorn. What size did he buy?   _____

4. The movie is 1 hour and 30 minutes long. If the class goes to the 10:00 A.M. movie, what time will it end?
   a. 10:30 A.M.
   b. 11:00 A.M.
   c. 11:30 A.M.
   d. 12:00 P.M.   _____

5. The second grade needed to buy 7 additional tickets. How much did they pay?   _____

6. There are 75 students and 4 teachers in your grade level. How many tickets will your school need to pay for?   _____

7. The parent volunteer for the second grade paid $12.00 for additional tickets. How many tickets did she buy?   _____

8. Half of the second graders went to the movie for free. How many students are in second grade?   _____

Let's Go to the Movies

The Picture:
The picture is a movie poster/advertisement. There is a star burst announcing school discounts and ticket prices. There are popcorn and soda prices listed. There are three show times for the movie.

Teacher Notes:
Students see advertisements everywhere they go. They may see specials at grocery stores, billboards selling cars, or commercials on TV. The movie poster is targeting schools with its food discounts, ticket discounts, and show times during the school day.

Explain to students that discounts allow them to save money. To see how much money can be saved, have students figure out the full price of an item, then have them subtract the amount of the discounted price.

When adding money amounts, make sure students line up decimal points before adding and subtracting.

When adding an amount of time to a given time, have students add the minutes before adding the hours.

Extension Activities:
1. Plan a class trip to the movies or another show, such as a concert or play. Have students determine the price per student if tickets are $2.00 and the bus transportation fee is $1.50. Challenge students by telling them additional information, such as, "the PTA donated half of the bus fee" or, "the first 20 students pay full price; all additional students pay half price."
2. Collect various advertisements for shows in your area. Have students compare costs and determine which is the best bargain.
3. Have students write persuasive letters to the manager of a movie theater to ask for free tickets to a specific movie that has been approved by the school administration and parents.
4. Make a bar or pictograph of students' favorite movies.
5. Ask a local movie theater to donate empty popcorn containers, at least one of each size. While you are in the movie theater, note how much each size costs and write it on the appropriate container. Then, go to a local store and purchase different popcorn varieties: already popped in a bag, microwave popcorn, and unpopped kernels. Determine how many of each size container can be filled with each store-bought popcorn. Compare prices from the grocery store brands and the movie theater popcorn to see how much money the theater makes from each container of popcorn. Let students determine which of the store-bought varieties is the most economical.
6. Have students make a Venn diagram comparing watching a movie in a theater versus at home.

Vanilla Cake
$1.00 per slice

Cinnamon Loaf
$1.00 per slice

Fudge   25¢ each

Small Chocolate
Cupcakes

Chocolate Cookies
50¢ each or 3 for $1.00

Italian Pizzelle
Cookies   50¢ each

Fudge Brownies
2 for $1.00 or 60¢ each

Chocolate Chip
Cookies   50¢ each

Large Chocolate
Cupcakes   50¢ each

BAKE SALE
10:00 – NOON

© Carson-Dellosa • CD-104023

Name _____

A Sweet Fund-Raiser

Use the bake sale items to answer the questions.

1. How many different items were sold
    at the bake sale?   _____

2. Gina sold 6 Italian pizzelle cookies. How much
    money did she make?   _____

3. Small cupcakes cost half the price of large
    cupcakes. How much are small cupcakes?   _____

4. Virginia bought a piece of fudge and a large
    cupcake. How much did she spend?   _____

5. Fred wants to buy all of the plates of brownies
    and cupcakes. How many plates will be left on
    the table after Fred's purchase?   _____

6. How long did the bake sale last?
    a. 1 hour
    b. 2 hours
    c. 5 hours   _____

CD-104023 • Real-World Math

Name _____

A Sweet Fund-Raiser

Use the bake sale items to answer the questions.

1. There are petals on each pizzelle cookie. If there are 2 pizzelle cookies on a plate, how many petals are there? _____

2. All of the items on the top row were sold. These plates were taken away. How many plates are left on the table? _____

3. If Ryan buys 2 brownies, how much less will he pay for each brownie? _____

4. When Mrs. Jones cuts the vanilla cake, she will cut along the lines. How much would it cost to buy every slice of the cake? _____
    a. $4.00
    b. $5.00
    c. $16.00 _____

5. If Jenny sold a dozen pieces of fudge, how much money did she make? _____

6. Mrs. Hill counted the large chocolate cupcakes that are left on the table. She baked 18 cupcakes. How many did she sell? _____

7. Kelly cut the cinnamon loaf into 8 slices. How much did she make by selling half of the loaf? _____

8. George wants to buy one of each item that has to be sliced. How many items can he buy? _____

A Sweet Fund-Raiser

The Picture:
The picture is a school bake sale. The following baked goods can be seen on the table from left to right:
First Row: chocolate chip cookies, Italian pizzelle cookies, small chocolate cupcakes, vanilla cake (8 large sections, 8 small sections)
Second Row: large chocolate cupcakes, chocolate cookies, cinnamon loaf
Third Row: fudge brownies, fudge

Teacher Notes:
Students will often see bake sales at school or church. Explain that people donate baked goods and a group sells them to raise money.

Bring in several baking pans and recipes to show students. There are muffin tins available that make six muffins or one dozen. Most cookie recipes have serving sizes in dozens. Explain that a dozen equals 12.

When teaching younger students money skills, use money manipulatives for better understanding. Display a money equivalent chart on a bulletin board so that students know when to trade multiple coins for single coins with greater values.

When teaching students time, use a clock with moveable hands that shows the hour hand move as the minute hand advances.

When introducing the concept of one half, tell students that it is the same thing as making a fair share for two people.

Extension Activities:
1. Talk to students about different fund-raisers they have participated in by either selling items or buying items. Which fund-raisers were most successful? Which types of items sold the best?
2. Have students set a goal for a fund-raiser. Encourage parents to donate baked goods to the school for a fund-raiser. Have students sell the items at the next PTA meeting. Use the money students raise to donate something to the school like math manipulatives, art supplies, a musical instrument, or books for the library.
3. Have parents donate snacks. Let students sample the snacks. Then, give each student a self-stick note. Write the names of the snacks across the bottom of the board. Let each student write his name on his self-stick note and place it above the name of his favorite snack. When the graph is complete, have students evaluate the favorite and least favorite snacks. (Before completing any food activity, ask families' permission and inquire about students' food allergies and religious or other food preferences.)
4. Bring in various baking pans that might have been used to make the desserts in the bake sale picture. Let students match the cookies, cakes, or loaves to the corresponding baking pans.

Yard Sale Today
Saturday, May 30
7:00 a.m. – Noon

Adult Clothes $2.00
Children's Clothes $1.00
All Toys   50¢
All Books $1.00
Flowerpots   25¢
Other items are
priced as marked.
Everything ½ off at 11:30.

Name _____

Yard Sale Today

Use the yard sale items to answer the questions.

1. Which items are the same price?
    a. toys and books
    b. flowerpots and toys
    c. children's clothes and books   _____

2. Mom set up the yard sale 1 hour before it began.
    What time did she start setting up?   _____

3. Hanna wanted to buy a stuffed penguin.
    It was 9:00 A.M. How much did she pay for it?   _____

4. David's mom bought a skirt and a book for herself
    at 8:12 A.M. How much did she spend?   _____

5. The lamp cost $1.00 more than an adult shirt. How
    much was the lamp at 11:15 A.M.?   _____

6. Sally bought a toy at 12:00 P.M. How much did she
    pay for her toy?
    a. 25¢
    b. 50¢
    c. $1.00   _____

7. Jared sold 4 of his old books and 2 toys before
    10:00 A.M. How much money did he make?   _____

CD-104023 • Real-World Math

Name _____

Yard Sale Today

Use the yard sale items to answer the questions.

1. Joli bought the purse for $5.00 at the yard sale.
    She also bought 2 books. How much did she pay
    altogether if it was before 11:30 A.M.?   _____

2. Jerry bought the rubber ball at 9:45 A.M. He paid
    with a dollar bill. How much change did he get?   _____

3. The beach towel had a price tag that said $2.00.
    How much did the beach towel cost after 11:30 A.M.? _____

4. Customers started to come to the yard sale
    30 minutes before it was scheduled to start. What
    time did people start coming to the sale?
    a. 6:00 A.M.
    b. 6:30 A.M.
    c. 7:30 A.M.   _____

5. How many minutes did it take Mrs. Harris to set
    up her yard sale if she finished at 6:45 A.M. and
    started at 6:05 A.M.?   _____

6. Stacey bought the penguin, the ball, a flowerpot, and
    2 books early in the morning. What was her total?
    a. $3.25
    b. $3.50
    c. $3.75   _____

7. Leah saved $4.00 from her allowance to spend
    at the yard sale. She bought 2 stuffed animals,
    a doll, a shirt, and a sweater, all before 11:00 A.M.
    How much money does she have left?   _____

Yard Sale Today

The Picture:
The picture is an outdoor yard sale. There is a sign that lists the hours of the yard sale and the prices of certain items.

Teacher Notes:
At yard sales, church bazaars, and flea markets, people are able to buy previously owned goods at reduced prices.

Teach students about bargaining. Explain that at a store, there are set prices for items. At a yard sale, a price may be reduced if a person bargains. *Bargaining* is when the buyer offers a price to the seller. The seller may accept the price offered or suggest another price. Usually the price agreed upon between buyer and seller is lower than the original price.

Have students practice underlining the important information in problems so that they can easily write number sentences. Display a poster with key addition terms, such as *altogether*, *total*, and *in all*. Then, make one with key subtraction terms, such as *left*, *spend*, *change* (money), *fewer*, and *more*. Demonstrate underlining the words and naming the rule before answering a problem.

Review calendar patterns. Explain that students should add seven to figure out one week later and subtract seven to figure out one week earlier.

When teaching students time, use a clock with moveable hands that shows the hour hand moving as the minute hand advances.

Extension Activities:
1. Have a school rummage sale to raise money. Send home a letter asking for donations for the rummage sale. Specify that all items should be in good condition and clean. Have students help you price the items. Talk with them about how much things are worth and how much people will pay. Use the money raised to buy something for the school or classroom.
2. Let students earn "classroom bucks" for good behavior. Bring in inexpensive items for them to buy with their classroom money. Have parents donate items to save money.
3. Discuss with students reasons a person might have a yard sale. Is he moving? Has he outgrown certain items? Does he need room for new items? Does he need to earn money?
4. Read *How the Second Grade Got $8,205.50 to Visit the Statue of Liberty* by Nathan Zimelman (Albert Whitman & Company, 1992) and *Yard Sale!* by Mitra Modarressi (Dorling Kindersley Publishing, 2000). Have students compare the two books in a Venn diagram.

Answer Key

The Beads Go On
Page 6
1. Jimmy
2. c.
3. 8
4. 4
5. 25¢
6. Answers may vary. Check for ABBC pattern.

Page 7
1. 4
2. a.
3. 10
4. 4
5. 12
6. b.
7. 6

Join the PTA!
Page 10
1. 16
2. yes
3. 17
4. $32.00
5. first grade
6. third
7. 12
8. a.

Page 11
1. c.
2. 11
3. odd
4. kindergarten
5. 65
6. 1st and 3rd
7. $60.00

Calendar Capers
Page 14
1. Tuesday
2. 3
3. February 9
4. February 23
5. 4
6. March
7. February 19
8. February 7

Page 15
1. 8
2. Thursday
3. February 25
4. 9 days
5. Monday
6. no
7. November 24

What Did You Do at School?
Page 18
1. Math Club
2. 1:00
3. 10:00
4. Room 14
5. art
6. c.
7. 1 hour

Page 19
1. Chess Club
2. 30 minutes
3. 30 minutes
4. 1 hour
5. 4 hours
6. 2.5 hours

Answer Key

Doughnuts for Dads
Page 22

1.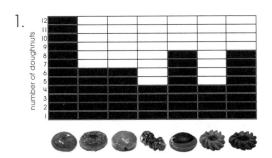

2. 10
3. with center holes

Page 23

1. $\frac{1}{4}$
2. 2
3. 1:2 (or 1 out of 2)
4. 48
5. 24
6. 41

How's the Weather?
Page 26

1. 1°F
2. 2
3. 8:00 P.M.
4. Friday
5. b.
6. b.
7. Minneapolis

Page 27

1. $\frac{1}{5}$
2. d.
3. 22°F; 12°C
4. 19°F; 11°C
5. 52 minutes

Get Your Lemonade
Page 30

1. b.
2. 2 hours
3. 15
4. 2:15
5. 4
6. d.
7. 4
8. large

Page 31

1. 15
2. large and small
3. small
4. no
5. b.
6. 3; 6; 12

What's for Lunch?
Page 34

1. 7
2. 3
3. grilled cheese sandwich
4. 15¢
5. hot dog
6. $1.50
7. chicken strips
8. c.

Page 35

1. $2.50
2. 3
3. $6.50
4. no
5. $1.25
6. a.
7. a.

Answer Key

Do Your Chores
Page 38
1. 7
2. Rake leaves in front yard.
3. $2.00
4. 50¢
5. b.
6. $1.25
7. Lauren

Page 39
1. c.
2. $3.00
3. $1.50
4. 6 times
5. $4.75
6. d.
7. Matt

What Should I Wear?
Page 42
1. 3
2. 2
3. 2
4. $2.00
5. b.
6. 50¢

Page 43
1. $3.00
2. 2
3. $10.00
4. no
5. 25¢
6. d.

Yummy Fruit Pizza
Page 46
1. 6
2. b.
3. 3 minutes
4. 8 ounces
5. 2
6. 190°C
7. 6

Page 47
1. 600
2. 32
3. 1 cup
4. 80 grams
5. 3
6. 2 cups
7. 50°F

Let's Go to the Movies
Page 50
1. 8:00 A.M.
2. 2 hours
3. 50¢
4. medium popcorn
5. 10; $20.00
6. $15.00
7. 10:00 A.M.

Page 51
1. 25¢
2. $15.00
3. medium
4. c.
5. $14.00
6. 25
7. 6
8. 100

Answer Key

A Sweet Fund-Raiser
Page 54
1. 9
2. $3.00
3. 25¢
4. 75¢
5. 6
6. b.

Page 55
1. 12
2. 5
3. 10¢
4. c.
5. $3.00
6. 13
7. $4.00
8. 2

Yard Sale Today
Page 58
1. c.
2. 6:00 A.M.
3. 50¢
4. $3.00
5. $3.00
6. a.
7. $5.00

Page 59
1. $7.00
2. 50¢
3. $1.00
4. b.
5. 40 minutes
6. a.
7. 50¢

CD-104023 • Real-World Math